The Properties of Metals

Marylou Morano Kjelle

Rosen
Classroom

To my nephew and niece, Zachary Scott and Jessica Marie Mongold

Published in 2007 by The Rosen Publishing Group, Inc.
29 East 21st Street, New York, NY 10010

First Edition

Editors: Daryl Heller, Joanne Randolph, Suzanne Slade
Book Design: Elana Davidian
Layout Design: Ginny Chu
Photo Researcher: Marty Levick

Photo Credits: Cover © E. Streichan/zefa/Corbis; pp. 5, 11 Charles D. Winters/Photo Researchers, Inc.; p. 7 Mark A. Schneider/Photo Researchers, Inc.; pp. 8, 10 Andrew Lambert Photography/Photo Researchers, Inc.; p. 9 Martin Bond/Photo Researchers, Inc.; p. 13 © Turbo/zefa/Corbis; p. 14 © Bettmann/Corbis; p. 15 James L. Amos/Peter Arnold, Inc.; p. 16 © LWA-Stephen Welstead/Corbis; p. 17 Sisse Brimberg/National Geographic Image Collection; p. 18 © Greg Pease/Stone/Getty Images; p. 19 © Mikhail Lavrenov/istockphoto; p. 20 © Layne Kennedy/Corbis; p. 21 © Images.com/Corbis.

Library of Congress Cataloging-in-Publication Data

Kjelle, Marylou Morano.
   The properties of metals / Marylou Morano Kjelle.— 1st ed.
      p. cm. — (The library of physical science)
   Includes index.
   ISBN 1-4042-3417-9 (library binding) — ISBN 1-4042-2164-6 (pbk.) — ISBN 1-4042-2354-1 (six pack)
   1. Metals—Juvenile literature. 2. Matter—Properties—Juvenile literature. I. Title. II. Series.

QD171.K566 2007
546'.3—dc22

                                        2005032937

Manufactured in the United States of America

Contents

Metals Are Natural Matter

What does a penny have in common with a soda can? They are both made of metal. There are many different kinds of metals. Most share some physical properties. Physical properties are things you can measure and see, such as color, shape, or hardness.

The Periodic Table of Elements

H																	He
Li	Be											B	C	N	O	F	Ne
Na	Mg											Al	Si	P	S	Cl	Ar
K	Ca	Sc	Ti	V	Cr	Mn	Fe	Co	Ni	Cu	Zn	Ga	Ge	As	Se	Br	Kr
Rb	Sr	Y	Zr	Nb	Mo	Tc	Ru	Rh	Pd	Ag	Cd	In	Sn	Sb	Te	I	Xe
Cs	Ba	La	Hf	Ta	W	Re	Os	Ir	Pt	Au	Hg	Tl	Pb	Bi	Po	At	Rn
Fr	Ra	Ac	Rf	Db	Sg	Bh	Hs	Mt	Uun	Uuu	Uub	Uut	Uuq	Uup	Uuh	Uus	Uuo

Ce	Pr	Nd	Pm	Sm	Eu	Gd	Tb	Dy	Ho	Er	Tm	Yb	Lu
Th	Pa	U	Np	Pu	Am	Cm	Bk	Cf	Es	Fm	Md	No	Lr

Metals make up three-quarters of the elements on the periodic table. Metals here are the elements colored blue, orange, red, and green.

On the periodic table of elements, metals are broken into three groups. These are alkali, alkaline earth, and transition metals. About three-fourths of the elements on Earth are metals. Elements are the basic **substances** that create everything in the world.

Iron is a silvery gray metal that is listed on the periodic table as Fe. People use iron to make many useful tools and other metals, such as steel.

Metals are found throughout nature. Some metals, such as sodium, are found in the ocean's waters. Calcium is a metal that people need to eat to build strong bones and teeth. Did you know that tiny pieces of metal are also floating in the air? When you take a breath, you are breathing metals!

Metals Have Luster

Elements are made of tiny parts called atoms. Atoms are made of electrons, protons, and neutrons. Protons and neutrons make up the nucleus, or center, of the atom. Electrons move around the nucleus in groups called clouds.

The electrons that are farthest from the nucleus give a metal its shine. Light reflects, or **bounces** off, these outer electrons. This makes the metal appear shiny.

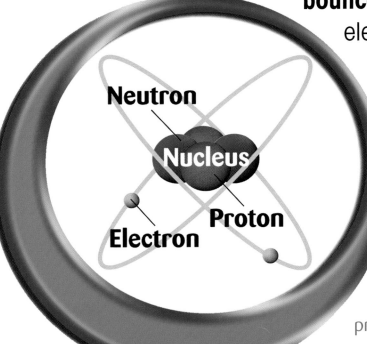

Neutron

Nucleus

Proton

Electron

Neutrons and protons make up the nucleus of an atom, as shown here. Electrons spin around the nucleus. Gold has 79 electrons, 79 protons, and 118 neutrons.

Many people prize gold for its beautiful luster and its ability to be formed into thin shapes.

This shiny appearance on the surface of some metals is called luster. People make **jewelry** out of gold and silver because these metals have a beautiful shiny luster.

Polishing a piece of metal increases its luster. This is because polishing removes **particles** that form on the surface of the metal over time. These particles form as the metal's surface **reacts** to **oxygen** and water in the **environment**. These particles do not reflect light well, and the metal appears dull.

Metals Are Strong Solids

Do you know what makes most metals solid? As with all solid matter, most metals' atoms are bonded tightly together. These strong bonds hold the atoms in a rigid, or stiff, pattern. A metal will not flow, pour, or move on its own because of its tight bonds.

Most metals are strong, but different metals have different strengths. For example, iron is a strong metal. It takes great force or heat

The liquid drops shown here are liquid mercury. Mercury is used in thermometers because it expands, or gets bigger, when heated. It contracts, or gets smaller, when cooled. A thermometer is used to tell how hot or cold something is.

This bridge is made of iron. Iron is a strong metal. It rusts, or breaks down, when air and water touch it, though. Today iron is often mixed with other metals so that it will not rust so easily.

to change iron's shape. Many tools are made using iron and other metals. A metal called aluminum is not as strong as iron. You can change the shape of an aluminum soda can by stepping on it.

Almost all metals are solid at room **temperature**. Mercury is the only metal that is a liquid at this low temperature. Mercury can flow.

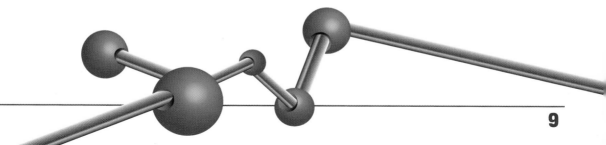

Metals Conduct Electricity

Electricity is a type of **energy**. People use electricity to make light and heat in their homes. Electricity also provides power for things like your computer and television. Most metals can conduct, or move, electricity from one place to another. A metal's ability to conduct electricity depends on its outer electrons. In most metals the outer electrons are loosely bonded to the atom. When an

Lightning rods, like the one on this building, are often made from copper. The electricity from lightning is drawn to the rod, instead of to the building. The rod carries the electricity down to the ground safely.

electrical force meets a metal, the metal's outer electrons leave one atom and join another atom in the metal. This continues to happen and the electricity is carried from one place to another.

Copper is a good conductor of electricity. Not all metals conduct electricity as well as copper does. For example, the electrons in brass do not move as easily as those in copper do. However, brass is still a better conductor than many other **materials**, such as rubber, paper, and wood.

Copper wiring is stored on spools. Copper wire can be found in most homes or buildings. The wire carries electricity to the different rooms in a building. This provides power for lights and appliances.

Metals Conduct Heat

Most metals that are good conductors of electricity are also good conductors of heat. When a metal is heated, some of its outer electrons absorb, or take in, the heat and begin to move more freely. When this happens they **collide** with cooler outer electrons nearby. The heat transfers, or moves, from the hot electrons to the cooler ones. In this way heat

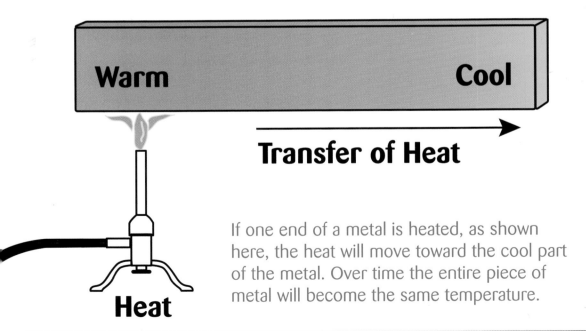

Warm

Cool

Transfer of Heat

Heat

If one end of a metal is heated, as shown here, the heat will move toward the cool part of the metal. Over time the entire piece of metal will become the same temperature.

Pots and pans are made of metals such as aluminum or copper. When a pot is placed on a hot burner on a stove, the heat moves from the part of the pan on the burner to the rest of the pan. This property lets us heat foods evenly.

is moved from one part of a metal to another.

Metals, such as copper and aluminum, are good heat conductors. They are used to make pots and pans for cooking food. However, many other metals are not as good at conducting heat. Their outer electrons do not move around as much, so they conduct heat slowly.

Metals Are Malleable

Some metals can be pressed or bent into different shapes without breaking. This physical property is called malleability. Like those in other solids, a metal's atoms are packed tightly together. A force, such as the pounding of a hammer, can move the atoms in some metals.

Aluminum is an example of a malleable metal. It can be pressed into thin sheets, which can easily be formed into different shapes. The

The ability of metal to be made in different shapes is a very useful property. Steel can be shaped into long beams that are used to build buildings. Here the Empire State Building in New York City is being built. You can see the many beams that make its frame strong.

aluminum foil you use to cover foods is a very thin sheet of aluminum. Silver and gold are also malleable metals.

People work with malleable metals and metal **alloys** in different ways. A coppersmith makes copper items, such as pots and pans. Builders use the strong metal alloy called steel to make bridges and buildings. The malleability of metals is just one of their useful properties.

Aluminum can be pressed into flat sheets. These thin sheets of metal can be used in making cars, airplanes, cans, and many other useful items.

Metals Are Ductile

When you picture a metal, you probably think of it as a block or a chunk. Yet some metals can be pulled, or drawn, and made longer and thinner. This physical property is called ductility. Ductile metals are used to make objects such as paper clips and wire.

Some metals become softer when they are heated. The softer a metal becomes, the more ductile it is.

Paper clips are made by heating a metal until it becomes ductile. The heated metal can be pulled into a long thin wire. Then it is bent into a clip.

These necklaces are made from gold, which is a very ductile metal. Gold has been used since ancient times to make jewelry.

As the metal is softened and shaped into a wire, the bonds holding the atoms together break apart. New bonds will form once the metal cools. These new bonds allow metal to keep its new shape.

Gold is a very ductile metal. It is often used to make fine necklaces and earrings. Gold can be stretched and twisted into decorative shapes without breaking. Some metals and alloys, such as hard steel, are not as ductile. When their shape is changed too greatly, they crack, or break.

Melting and Boiling Metals

All metals will melt when heated. When a metal melts, it turns from a solid into a liquid. The temperature at which this first occurs is called a metal's melting point. Most metals have high melting points. This is because of the strong bonds holding the metal's atoms together. It takes a lot of energy to loosen the bonds so that the metal can become a liquid. Because many metals have high

When a metal melts we call it molten. Here a large pot of molten steel is being poured.

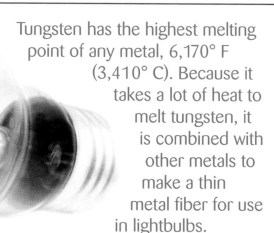

Tungsten has the highest melting point of any metal, 6,170° F (3,410° C). Because it takes a lot of heat to melt tungsten, it is combined with other metals to make a thin metal fiber for use in lightbulbs.

melting points, they are often used to make objects that are put in very hot places. For example, the parts inside an airplane engine must stay strong and not melt when temperatures get hot.

If a metal is heated to a high enough temperature, the bonds holding the atoms together finally break down completely. Bubbles form at the liquid's bottom, rise to its surface, and escape into the atmosphere as a gas. The temperature at which a metal turns into a gas is called the metal's boiling point.

Ready, Set, React!

Metals are strong. When some metals react with certain elements, though, they break down and become weak. Have you ever noticed rust on an old car or on a grill that has been left outside for a long time? Rust forms when the iron in an object reacts with water or oxygen. When water **molecules** hit the surface of the iron, a new **compound** called ferric oxide, or rust, is created.

This old car is rusting. If iron is left in a wet place too long, the metal will completely break down.

Metals make for a beautiful fireworks display. Magnesium and aluminum produce white sparks. Calcium salts are used to create orange lights, and copper produces blue colors.

Silver also reacts with other elements. Silver's outer layer turns dark as it reacts with **sulfur** or with the oxygen in the air. This dark coloring is called tarnish.

Did you know that if metals did not react with other elements, we would not be able to enjoy fun events like fireworks displays? The flashes of color you see in fireworks are caused by the dust from different metals reacting with the other matter in a firework. The next time you watch a beautiful fireworks display, you can thank metals!

A Matter of Time

People have used metals since ancient times. **Archaeologists** know that early peoples used gold to make **utensils** and iron to make tools and weapons.

Throughout the centuries the use of metals continued to grow. New inventions needing metals, including the telephone and the lightbulb, were created. Today the businesses that build automobiles and airplanes make use of the properties of metals and combined metals.

Most of the 86 known metals were discovered in the last 100 years. Americium is a humanmade metal that was created in Chicago in 1944. The smoke detector in your house and school use americium to help save lives. The properties of metals make them useful in so many ways. Can you imagine a world without metals?

Glossary

alloys (A-loyz) Substances composed of two or more elements.

archaeologists (ar-kee-AH-luh-jists) People who study the remains of peoples from the past to understand how they lived.

bounces (BOWNS-ez) Springs up, down, or to the side.

collide (kuh-LYD) To crash together.

compound (KOM-pownd) Two or more things combined.

energy (EH-nur-jee) The power to work or to act.

environment (en-VY-ern-ment) All the living things and conditions of a place.

jewelry (JOO-ul-ree) Objects worn for decoration that are made of special metals, such as gold and silver, and prized stones.

materials (muh-TEER-ee-ulz) What something is made of.

molecules (MAH-lih-kyoolz) The smallest bits of matter possible before they can be broken down into their basic parts.

oxygen (OK-sih-jen) A gas that has no color, taste, or odor and is necessary for people and animals to breathe.

particles (PAR-tih-kulz) Pieces of something.

polishing (PAH-lish-ing) Making smooth or shiny by rubbing.

reacts (ree-AKTs) Goes through a chemical change when put with other matter.

substances (SUB-stans-ez) Any matter that takes up space.

sulfur (SUL-fer) A nonmetallic element that often forms yellow crystals.

temperature (TEM-pur-cher) How hot or cold something is.

utensils (yoo-TEN-sulz) Tools usually used in cooking or eating.

Index

Web Sites

Due to the changing nature of Internet links, PowerKids Press has developed an online list of Web sites related to the subject of this book. This site is updated regularly. Please use this link to access the list:
www.powerkidslinks.com/lops/metals/